THEOTOKOS ICONS COLORING BOOK

HOPE AND LIFE PRESS

First published in 2017 by
HOPE AND LIFE PRESS

Theotokos Icons Coloring Book

Copyright © 2017 Hope and Life Press – All rights reserved.

Published by
HOPE AND LIFE PRESS
2312 Chemin Herron #A, Dorval QC, H9S 1C5 Canada; and
P.O. Box 37, East Longmeadow, MA 01028, USA.
http://hopeandlifepress.com
hopeandlifepress@gmail.com

All rights reserved. No part of this work may be reproduced, stored in a retrieval system, or submitted in any form or by any means, electronic, mechanical, photocopying, recording or otherwise, without the prior written permission of the publisher. This book may not be lent, resold, hired out or otherwise disposed of by way of trade in any form of binding or cover other than that in which it is published, without the prior written consent of the published.

Printed in the United States of America.

CONTENTS

THEOTOKOS ICONS COLORING BOOK

The Theotokos	5
The Annunciation	6
The Nativity	7
Detail of the Nativity	8
Tenderness	9
Do Not Tell Them, Mother	10
Ark of the Covenant	11
The Mother	12
The Mother and the Son	13
The Holy Family	14
Our Lady with the Child Jesus	15
More Tenderness	16
The Queen of Heaven	17
Our Lady of Perpetual Help	18
The Woman	19
Our Lady of Springfield	20
Source of Life	21
The Mother-Queen	22
Here is My Son	23
The Beauty of the Theotokos	24
Select Books of Hope and Life Press	25

The Theotokos

THE ANNUNCIATION

THE NATIVITY

DETAIL OF THE NATIVITY

TENDERNESS

Ark of the Covenant

The Mother

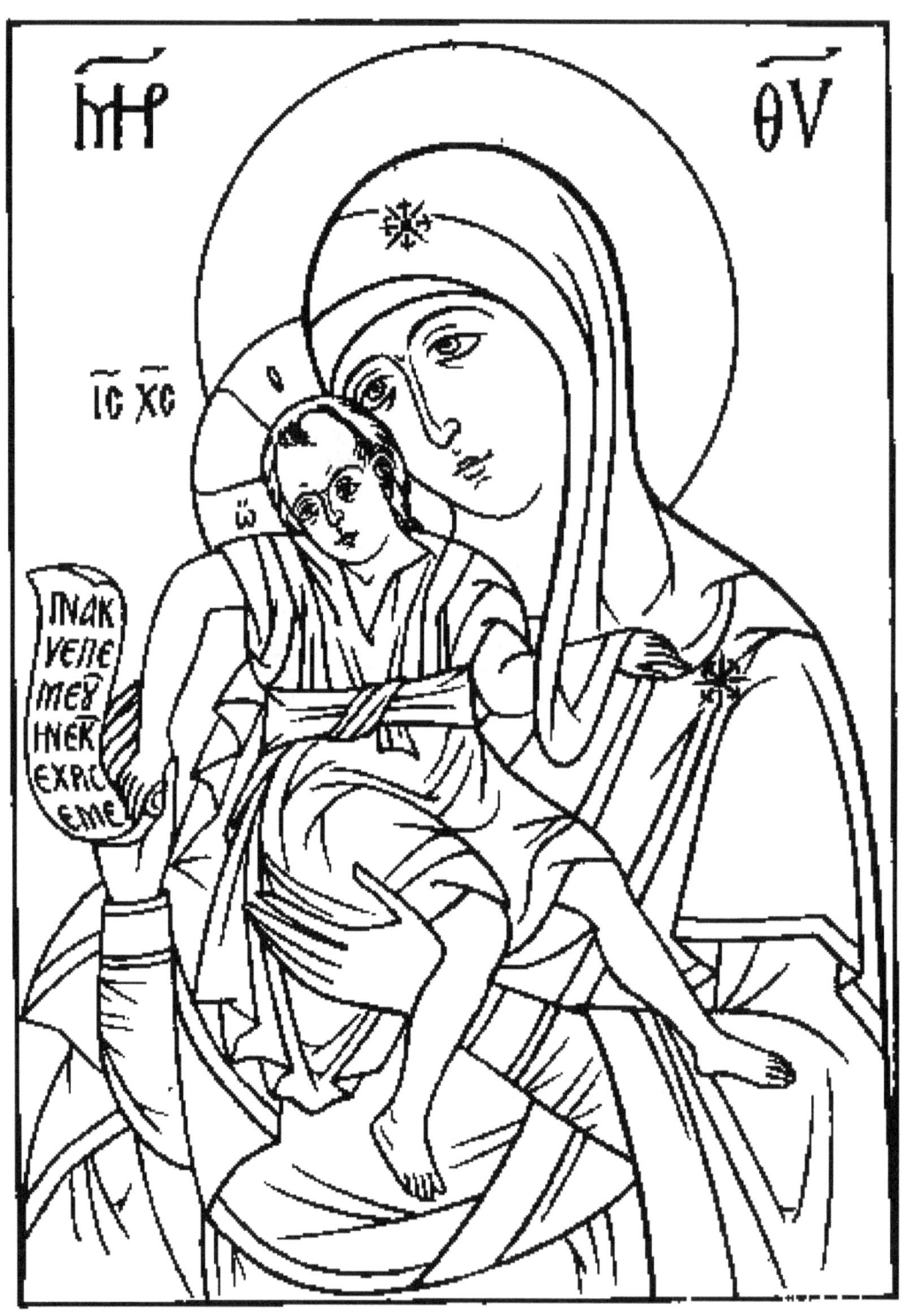

The Mother and the Son

The Holy Family

Our Lady with the Child Jesus

More Tenderness

The Queen of Heaven

Our Lady of Perpetual Help

THE WOMAN

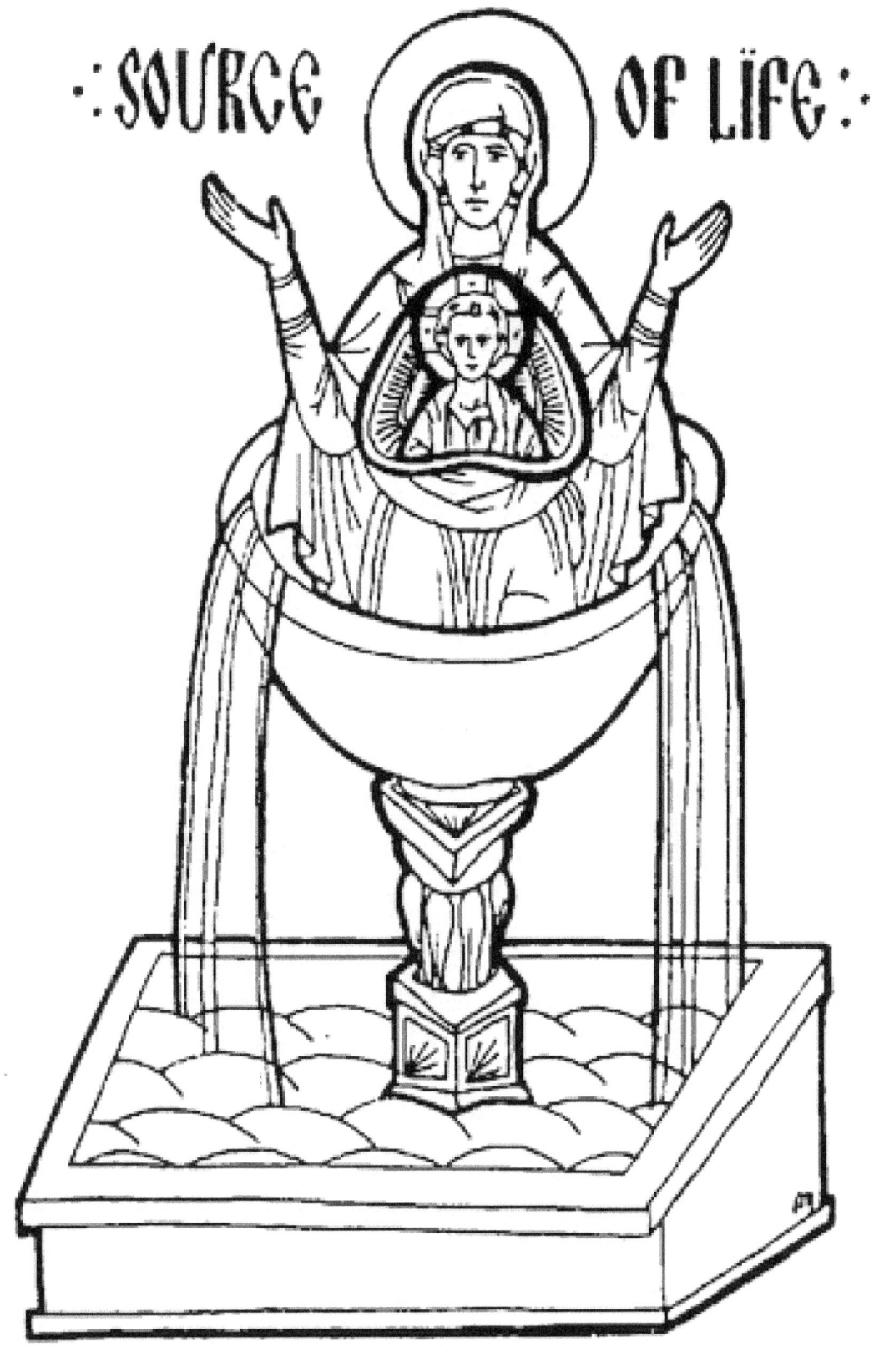

THE MOTHER-QUEEN

Here is My Son

Select Books of Hope and Life Press

  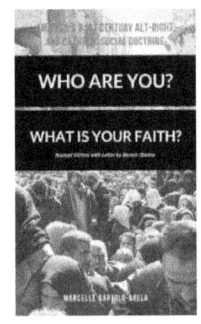  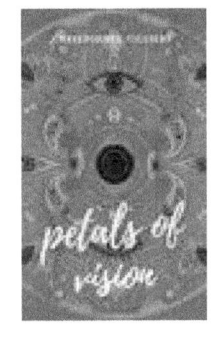

    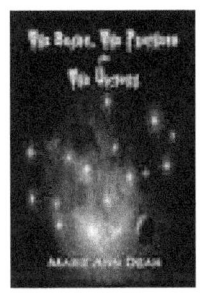

    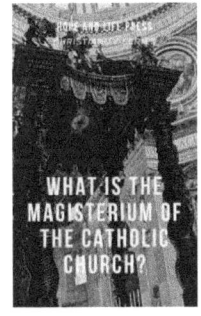

  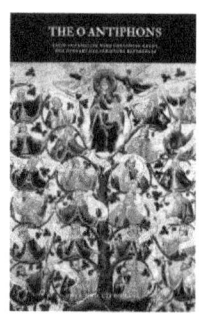 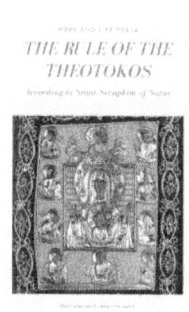

www.ingramcontent.com/pod-product-compliance
Lightning Source LLC
Chambersburg PA
CBHW080416300426
44113CB00015B/2545